GENERATIVE AI
IN THE
CLASSROOM

GENERATIVE AI IN THE CLASSROOM

{ Laura Knight }

CORWIN

A SAGE Publishing Company

1 Oliver's Yard
55 City Road
London EC1Y 1SP

2455 Teller Road
Thousand Oaks
California 91320

Unit No 323-333, Third Floor, F-Block
International Trade Tower
Nehru Place, New Delhi – 110 019

8 Marina View Suite 43-053
Asia Square Tower 1
Singapore 018960

© 2025 Laura Knight

Apart from any fair dealing for the purposes of research or private study, or criticism or review, as permitted under the Copyright, Designs and Patents Act 1988, this publication may be reproduced stored or transmitted in any form, or by any means, only with the prior permission in writing of the publishers, or in the case of reprographic reproduction in accordance with the terms of licences issued by the Copyright Licensing Agency. Enquiries concerning reproduction outside those terms should be sent to the publishers.

Editor: Amy Thornton
Senior project editor: Chris Marke
Cover design: Wendy Scott
Typeset by: C&M Digitals (P) Ltd, Chennai, India
Printed and bound by
CPI Group (UK) Ltd, Croydon, CR0 4YY

Library of Congress Control Number: 2024944301

British Library Cataloguing in Publication data

A catalogue record for this book is available from the British Library

ISBN 978-1-0362-0079-4 (pbk)

TABLE OF CONTENTS

{ ABOUT THIS BOOK }

Generative AI has the potential to transform teaching by reducing workload, enhancing learning and fostering creativity. It also poses significant challenges and raises important questions. This book is for teachers who want to know more about Generative AI: how it works, the ethical questions it raises and what it can do for them and their students.

a little guide for teachers

{ ABOUT THE SERIES }

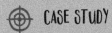 CASE STUDY

HINTS AND TIPS

REFLECTION

RESOURCES

IDEAS FOR THE CLASSROOM

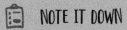 NOTE IT DOWN

www.sagepub.co.uk/littleguides

CASE STUDY 2.1

A WORKED EXAMPLE FOR A YEAR 10

You can start simple and gradu
that will flow beautifully togeth
for your class that fits perfectly
when you're working with a m
resources aren't pitched right,
isn't cutting it any more. Here
created to resource a KS4 Fre
introduce some vocabulary. I
use the new items is a piece

PROMPTS:

1. Create a vocabulary li
    theme of 'house and
    a mixture of nouns, v
    genders are included

NOTE IT DOWN

• WHAT DOES SUCCESSFUL LEARNING LOOK LIKE IN AN
  AI-INFUSED LESSON?

• THINKING YOURSELF INTO THE FUTURE, IMAGINE YOU
  ARE AN OBSERVER IN ONE OF YOUR OWN LESSONS,
  WATCHING YOURSELF TEACH A CLASS. DON'T BE
  TEMPTED TO GET TOO CAUGHT UP IN A SCI-FI FANTASY!
  LET'S KEEP THIS GROUNDED IN THE POSSIBLE.

• HOW IS GENAI HELPING YOU WITH ...?

  • PLANNING
  • RESOURCE CREATION
  • MARKING
  • ASSESSMENT
  • DATA AND INSIGHTS

ABOUT THE AUTHOR

Laura Knight MEd PGCE BA(Hons) FCCT FRSA CMgr *(she/they)*

Laura Knight is Founder of Sapio Ltd, an educational consultancy specialising in digital innovation. She was previously Director of Digital Learning at Berkhamsted School. She has been working as a teacher for 20 years and is an expert in leading the strategic development of technology for teaching and learning, 1–1 devices, artificial intelligence, staff training in digital skills and online safeguarding.

Laura is a disruptive thinker, international keynote speaker, coach and consultant, and is passionate about creative problem-solving. She supports educators in schools, universities and commercial organisations with exploring the art of the possible, and leverages technology to transform outcomes, systems and teams.

Laura works with the Independent Schools Council Digital Advisory Group and is a leading member of a national cross-sector working group on AI in education, with a keen interest in the future of education, digital wellbeing, safeguarding and regulation. She has also recently worked as an expert advisor to international governments on educational policy and provides expert input for associations such as the Independent Schools Association, the Society of Heads and the Independent Schools' Bursars' Association.

 linkedin.com/in/asklauraknight

INTRODUCTION

This is a straightforward, non-technical starting point for teachers who would like to find out more about Generative AI. This new technology has great potential to unlock transformative possibilities for education, and I hope the examples and information in these pages help teachers take their first steps with confidence. It is so important that we use the best that technology can offer us to support the learning of the young people we serve, and I am delighted you are here, investing your time and energy in that mission.

After 20 years in the classroom, and over ten of them specialising in digital education, I know just how powerful it can be when teachers leverage technology to amplify the impact of their subject knowledge, pedagogical skills and professional relationships with their students. I don't think for a moment that AI will replace teachers, but teachers who use it well may replace those who don't!

In Chapter 1 of this book, we will explore how to get started with Generative AI; there are lots of tips, ideas and worked examples to try out. In Chapter 2 we will look in more detail at how Generative AI can support teaching and learning; Chapter 3 will consider supporting pupils with SEND. Chapter 4 identifies how to inspire creativity and innovation both for teachers and pupils, and Chapter 5 reflects on the challenges and risks that come with this new technology in the educational context. Finally, in Chapter 6, we will unpack how to use Generative AI responsibly and ethically in schools, and how to prepare students for an AI-infused world.

Generative AI is undergoing fast-moving change and development, and we are in a period when identifying the potential value, trialling and then deploying it with the appropriate care is a challenge. I invite you to consider how to tread lightly but with purpose: there is no better time to engage with this new technology than now. Every time you have planning, researching, organising or reviewing to do, there will be new scope to extend your own capabilities and skills with technology in ways that did not exist before. That is exciting, and I hope you feel empowered to *be you, but better. Onwards!*

CHAPTER 1
GETTING STARTED
WITH GENERATIVE AI

This chapter covers:

- The concept of Generative AI and how it came into existence
- An overview of different types of Generative AI output
- How best to use prompts to achieve useful results for classroom practice
- The limitations of Generative AI technology

WHAT IS GENERATIVE AI, AND HOW DOES IT WORK?

Generative AI (GenAI) is a type of artificial intelligence that enables a computer system to produce new content from scratch. This could be text, music, code, images, video, audio, or data. The key here is that the AI isn't just copying or remixing existing materials. AI generates new creations. It does this by learning patterns from information it is trained on, and then applying those patterns in new ways.

Doesn't all AI do that? No. 'Artificial intelligence' is a term that was coined in the 1950s and is an umbrella term we use to talk about a whole cluster of technologies, including the natural language processing behind Alexa and Siri, the neural networks that create personalised recommendations for you on Netflix and Spotify, the computer vision that is used in facial recognition when you unlock your phone, or the robotics that are used in Roomba vacuum cleaners. While IBM's Deep Blue was powerful enough to beat Grand Master Garry Kasparov at chess in 1997, it was an example of Narrow AI: it couldn't play any other games, let alone give you the weather forecast. We won't dismiss Narrow AI though: we rely on this kind of technology to filter spam from our inbox and spot credit card fraud!

KEY TERMS

- **Large language model:** A type of AI that's trained on a vast amount of text data. It can generate human-like text based on the input or 'prompt' it's given.

- **Prompt:** The input or instruction given to an AI. It's like a question or command that tells the AI what you want it to do.

- **Training data:** The information AI learns from. For a language model, this could be a large amount of text data.

- **Chatbot:** A software application used to conduct an online chat conversation via text or text-to-speech, in lieu of providing direct contact with a live human agent.

- **Algorithm:** A set of instructions or rules that guides the process of learning from data, making predictions, or producing output.

WHAT CAN GenAI DO, AND HOW CAN IT HELP TEACHERS?

GenAI has the power to be a real help to teachers, to support many different aspects of our work.

It does not replace your professional skill, judgement, or relationships, but it can help with:

- **Planning and Organisation:** Generative AI can accelerate lesson planning, put curriculum content together, build outlines and streamline the organisation of events and trips.

- **Research:** AI aids in gathering and synthesising research information quickly.

- **Resources and Content Creation:** AI can create a wide range of educational resources and provides tailored explanations, questions, exercises and tasks.

- **Communications and Informational Writing:** It assists in creating clear and effective communication materials, such as newsletters, instructions, policies, summaries and lists.

- **Automating Processes:** It can accelerate feedback, assessment and marking, saving teachers' time.

- **Creativity:** It sparks creativity by generating novel ideas and materials for teaching.

- **Personalisation, Engagement and Adaptive Teaching:** AI personalises learning experiences, increases student engagement and adapts teaching methods to individual needs by helping teachers create multiple accessible versions of resources with ease.

Check out Chapter 2 for lots more information to help you get started.

WHAT ARE THE LIMITATIONS OF GenAI? WHAT CAN'T IT DO?

When faced with a new technology that people don't necessarily understand, it's tempting to give it magical abilities in our minds, but that is not a helpful approach. AI is not wizardry or witchcraft; and while it is powerful and developing all the time, it has its limitations. It is not capable of independent thought, reasoning, or action, and it can only do what it has been programmed to do. Understanding these limitations will help us use the tools more effectively and know which tool to choose for which task:

- **Lack of understanding:** While GenAI can produce outputs that seem quite human, they have no understanding of the content that they are producing, its meaning, whether it is true, accurate, or appropriate.

- **Rubbish in, rubbish out:** GenAI is only as good as the data it is trained on. If the training data is biased, incorrect, incomplete, or out of date the results you get will be flawed.

- **Unpredictability and inconsistency:** It's often hard to predict or control what a GenAI model will produce and that can lead to unexpected, inconsistent, or inappropriate outputs. This is especially important when we are using GenAI with students.

- **Blandness:** GenAI can mimic creativity, but it doesn't have human emotion, personal experience, worldview, or experiences which are the things that enrich genuine human communication. As a result, GenAI output can feel boringly neutral or even bland.

HOW CAN WE USE GENERATIVE AI EFFECTIVELY?

Using GenAI is definitely not rocket science. However, for the uninitiated it can seem intimidating, or the results might be underwhelming if we don't use a methodical approach to get the best outcomes. A methodical approach used to mitigate this is often called *prompt engineering*.

 HINTS AND TIPS 1.1

PROMPT ENGINEERING

Prompt engineering is the art of crafting effective prompts or inputs for a Generative AI model to get the desired output. It's becoming gradually less important as GenAI improves, but, for now, it's a skill we need to develop.

PROMPT ENGINEERING VS SEARCHING

Using GenAI is different to using a search engine: we are not asking the AI model to match what we are looking for with something that already exists. Instead, we are asking it to create a custom answer with new content.

 HINTS AND TIPS 1.2

KEY DEFINITIONS

A search engine like Google *retrieves* information, while Generative AI creates information.

To help you create brilliant results with GenAI, try using this structure for your prompts: *SCRIPT*.

Table 1.1 The SCRIPT prompt structure

S	*Specify*	Be specific about the task, and give details about the input you are going to provide as well as the output you want.
C	*Context*	Give clear information about the sector, subject, field, age-group, level of expertise, language, era and social/cultural context of the task.
R	*Role*	Explain who is the reader or audience, who is the writer and what their relationship is.
I	*Iterate*	Refine your output with tweaks and improvements over a series of drafts. Use feedback on each iteration to give pointers on how to make the output better.
P	*Parameters*	Tell the GenAI tool about the format you want for your output. Consider giving a word count, number of paragraphs, formatting information such as bullets, numbering, or style. Tell it about specialist language, timeframes, references, or case studies to include.
T	*Tone*	Adapt for reading level, formality, age-range, humour, optimism and whether the output should be persuasive, factual, creative, or procedural.

EXPERIMENTS TO TRY

Here are some experiments with GenAI to try. As with all new technologies, learning happens as you begin to use it. Note: I used Microsoft Copilot for these examples.

1. CREATIVE LAUNCHPAD

Ask your GenAI to create five different starting sentences for creative writing on the theme of your choice. Here are the outputs when I used this prompt on the theme of 'mystery':

Prompt: *Create five different starting sentences for creative writing on the theme of mystery.*

OUTPUT (AI GENERATED RESPONSE):

- Under the flickering lamplight, an old map revealed a path to the unknown.

- The moment the antique clock chimed midnight; a cryptic letter slid under my door.

- In the quiet town of Meadowgrove, everyone had a secret, but Mr. Hawthorne's was the most puzzling of all.

- As I stepped into the abandoned mansion, a chilling whisper echoed, hinting at a forgotten tale.

- The mirror, rumoured to show one's deepest desires, reflected an image I couldn't recognize.

2. ROLEPLAY Q+A

Ask your GenAI to act as interviewee in the role of a famous historical figure.

Prompt: *I am going to ask five questions, and you should answer them as if you were Henry VIII of England. Make your answers as factually accurate as possible. First question: what do you like to eat?*

OUTPUT (AI GENERATED RESPONSE):

As Henry VIII, I enjoyed grand feasts! My meals often included a variety of meats such as beef, mutton, and venison. I also enjoyed poultry, fish, fruits, and wine. However, my extravagant diet was not very balanced by today's standards. Now, what's your next question? ☺

3. POEM OR SONG

Ask GenAI to create a poem or song to help your students revise a tricky topic.

Prompt: *Create a rhyming poem about photosynthesis to help GCSE students revise key words and concepts.*

OUTPUT (AI GENERATED RESPONSE):

In leaves so green, the sun's light beams,
Photosynthesis, more than it seems.
Chlorophyll captures, water combines,
Carbon dioxide, in chloroplasts aligns.

```
Light reactions make ATP,
Calvin cycle sets glucose free.
Oxygen escapes, a breath of life,
Nature's answer to living strife.
```

4. EXPLANATION OF A CONCEPT

Ask GenAI to create an explanation of a concept you want to teach your students.

Prompt: *Write an explanation of how tectonic plates work in 100 words for a Year 6 Geography class.*

OUTPUT (AI GENERATED RESPONSE):

```
Tectonic plates are huge pieces of Earth's
crust that fit together like a jigsaw puzzle.
They float on a softer layer underneath and move
very slowly. Sometimes they slide past each
other, bump into one another, or move apart.
This can cause earthquakes, form mountains, or
create volcanoes. Imagine Earth's surface as a
cracked eggshell with each piece moving around
on the gooey egg white—that's how tectonic
plates work!
```

5. GENERATING QUESTIONS

Ask GenAI to write a list of multiple-choice questions to help you assess understanding.

Prompt: *Create five multiple-choice questions to check my students' understanding of when to use a semicolon in a sentence. Include plausible distractors and an answer key.*

OUTPUT (AI GENERATED RESPONSE):

1. When can you use a semicolon to join two related sentences?

   A) When they are complete opposites

   B) When they are independent clauses

   C) When one is a question

2. How do you use a semicolon in a list with complex items?

   A) To separate items that contain commas

   B) To start the list

   C) To end the list

3. Can you replace a conjunction with a semicolon? When?

   A) Yes, when connecting two dependent clauses

   B) No, never

   C) Yes, when connecting two independent clauses

4. What punctuation mark can you use before words like 'however' or 'therefore'?

   A) Comma

   B) Semicolon

   C) Exclamation mark

5. When should you not use a semicolon between two sentences?

   A) When they are unrelated

   B) When they are very short

   C) When they are questions

The correct answers are: 1-B, 2-A, 3-C, 4-B, 5-A

WHAT DOES THE FUTURE OF AI LOOK LIKE?

Many experts believe that the rise of AI is inevitable; Jürgen Schmidhuber, often referred to as the 'father of AI', has stated that 'You cannot stop it,' referring to the advancement of AI. He believes that AI will progress to the point where it surpasses human intelligence (Taylor, 2023).

There are lots of reasons why, as teachers, we should take Generative AI seriously and invest time into understanding it. One of our core purposes is to help children and young people flourish in the future, live fulfilling lives, contribute positively to society and achieve their potential. Generative AI will add trillions to the global economy each year and will play a considerable part in the future education and employment landscapes our students will experience. AI is evolving very rapidly and we can expect it to achieve human-level performance in some areas this decade. Understanding how we can harness this development to support human thriving will be a challenge we must all consider.

What about the future jobs our students will do? Will they change? Some sectors will be positively affected by AI, such as health and social care, education, technology and renewable energy, bringing growth and new opportunities. In other areas such as finance, clerical roles and manufacturing, we are likely to see a high rate of 'occupational substitution': where roles traditionally fulfilled by humans can more efficiently or more economically be done by AI (The Growth Summit: Jobs and Opportunity for All, 2024).

NOTE IT DOWN

- WHAT ARE THREE AREAS WHERE GENERATIVE AI COULD ASSIST OR STREAMLINE YOUR WORK, ESPECIALLY TASKS THAT CURRENTLY TAKE UP A LOT OF YOUR TIME?

  1.

  2.

  3.

- WHICH OF THE EXPERIMENTS COULD YOU ADAPT TO SUPPORT YOUR TEACHING?

- USING THE SCRIPT PROMPT ENGINEERING FRAMEWORK, CREATE A PROMPT TO HELP YOU PLAN AN UPCOMING LESSON.

CHAPTER 2
HOW CAN GENERATIVE AI SUPPORT TEACHING AND LEARNING?

This chapter covers:

- The potential of Generative AI specifically for education
- How Generative AI can save teacher time, boost engagement and raise student achievement
- Some strategies, practical tips and uses cases for using Generative AI
- Generating questions, feedback and assessments, creating learning materials, activities and projects

HOW CAN GenAI SAVE TEACHERS TIME IN THE CLASSROOM?

Teachers are busy people, and time is finite. Tools that help us speed up some of our routines, processes and workflows can be a real help, especially if that frees us up to ensure that the time we spend is having a positive impact on our students and colleagues.

Let's start by considering some of the visible, 'front of house' aspects of teaching and learning that can be accelerated or enhanced using GenAI.

- Accelerating lesson planning.

- Creating and adapting in-lesson activities, instructions, resources, quizzes and games.

- Developing discussion prompts, questions, experiments and exploratory scenarios.

- Building assignments, independent recall or practice, revision activities and homework tasks.

How can we do this? First, consider what your goals are for the lesson, unit, or activity. Defining the ideal outcome is a useful place to start and will help you be specific in your SCRIPT prompting.

 HINTS AND TIPS 2.1

SPECIFIC LEARNING OBJECTIVES

It's a good idea to give the GenAI your specific learning objectives, educational standards, outcomes, or goals, including the contextual information about where the students are in their learning.

Is this new learning, building on previous content, or revision? Do you want to assess understanding at the start, or at the end? What are the core skills you want to develop while working on the tasks you are creating? What does the ideal journey look like in terms of cognition, repetition, practice, recall, etc.? GenAI can support you in creating materials or adapting content that you already have, but it is a good idea to have a clear sense of where you want the students to end up.

RESOURCES 2.1

Check out magicschool.ai, teacherbot.io, diffit.me and teachmateai. com – they all have free versions. Why not compare them along with any other tools you are familiar with, by giving them all the same lesson resource creation prompt to see how the output varies. Which do you prefer? Why?

CASE STUDY 2.1

A WORKED EXAMPLE FOR A YEAR 10 FRENCH CLASS

You can start simple and gradually build up a suite of resources that will flow beautifully together and create a bespoke experience for your class that fits perfectly with your goals. This is a lifesaver when you're working with a new scheme of work, your existing resources aren't pitched right, are out of date, or the textbook just isn't cutting it any more. Here is an example of a series of prompts created to resource a KS4 French lesson where the teacher wants to introduce some vocabulary, practise it, and then have the students use the new items in a piece of independent writing.

PROMPTS

1. Create a vocabulary list for Year 10 French students on the theme of 'house and home'. Include 20 useful words with a mixture of nouns, verbs and adjectives. Ensure that the genders are included with the nouns.

(Continued)

2. Create a reading text describing a house using all these words, written in the present and perfect tenses by a young French person about their home. Include three opinion phrases. Add five comprehension questions in French with an answer key (adjust challenge level as needed).

3. Now create a cloze activity practising this vocabulary with ten questions connected to the reading text, and a second version with prompts in English for those who need additional support.

4. Build a ten-question grammar activity for students to practise possessive adjectives and agreement with nouns, using vocabulary from the previous activities. Add an answer key.

5. Create an independent writing task with five easy and five more challenging sentence starters provided for the students based on the same material, but for them to write about their own homes. Add a marking rubric and scoresheet so that students can peer assess each other's work based on language and communication.

6. Add a list of ten pieces of supplementary vocabulary for the students to use to boost the variety in their writing. Include some sophisticated words.

7. Build an exit ticket activity to complete this lesson and review the learning by creating a picture of a house with unusual features for students to describe. Make it colourful and playfully decorated.

This process might seem involved, but we can build a bespoke set of resources like this in less than ten minutes, which would have taken over an hour otherwise.

HINTS AND TIPS 2.2

EXISTING RESOURCES

You can use existing resources such as YouTube videos or pdfs as a starting point. This opens curriculum design up in new and exciting ways to innovation.

There is a balance to strike here: putting our time into change and development can feel like a risk, especially where current performance is at a good level. However, if we avoid trying new ideas, our practice can fossilise and that does not best serve the needs of our students in the longer term. Professional learning and experimentation are a good investment.

HOW CAN GenAI ENRICH THE LEARNING EXPERIENCE AND BOOST ENGAGEMENT FOR STUDENTS?

There is a lot more to GenAI's potential than rewriting what is in the textbook, and it would be a shame to leave our exploration there. Next, let's consider how we can use this technology to add new breadth, depth and inspiration to the curriculum. If we think about the Substitution, Augmentation, Modification and Redefinition (SAMR) model, this is where we are tipping into the modification and transformation of task design, allowing us to create new tasks and learning experiences that were previously inconceivable.

POWERFUL LEARNING PATHWAYS

- Personalised questioning based on mastery.
- Chatbots that mimic an expert tutor, trained on core content.
- Adaptive and responsive continuous assessment.
- Seamless stretch and challenge.
- Accessibility built-in.

INSPIRATIONAL EXPERIENCES

- Roleplay in fictional or historical contexts.

- Simulations and virtual worlds, such as ancient civilisations or distant planets.

- Making abstract concepts more tangible with live visualisations.

- Subject expertise in specialist areas.

BEYOND THE CLASSROOM

Now, let's also think about the less visible 'backstage' activities that can be supported using GenAI too:

- Drafting in-house and external communications, including to families.

- Planning for events, trips and co-curricular activities.

- Creating procedural and instructional writing.

How can we do this? As teachers, we spend a lot of time producing writing that supports the organisation and communications of school life. Much of the time, that is about making sure people know what they need to know. This could be information about trips and visits for parents, guidance for families on healthy nut-free snacks, a fundraising newsletter, requests for donations for a charity bake sale, or a script for an assembly about staying safe when walking home after dark. Using GenAI as a support, scaffold, drafting tool, sense-checker, or spelling, punctuation and grammar (SPAG) review on these types of communication can be incredibly helpful, especially when creating multiple versions of the same document for different age-groups, or languages.

 CASE STUDY 2.2

A WORKED EXAMPLE FOR A SCHOOL TRIP

Let's imagine a Year 6 residential trip is planned, and you are in charge. You will need to produce a letter for parents, an itinerary, briefing pack for the staff on the trip, a kit list, a medical form, a risk assessment, activities and games for the children, a code of conduct ... it's a lot, and this represents many hours of work on top of your teaching! Generative AI is the perfect companion to help you power through this quickly:

PROMPTS

1.   Create a letter to parents announcing the Year 6 residential trip to Kingswood, which will take place on 14–18 May. Introduce the location and types of activities in a positive and professional tone.

2.   Create a draft itinerary for each day including evening activities at Kingswood.

3.   Create a kit list of what each child should bring with them, including for wet weather.

4.   Create a template for a medical form for parents to sign and return including information about medications and conditions staff on the trip need to be aware of, and consent for emergency treatment.

5.   Create a staff handbook and schedule for the accompanying teachers on the trip.

6.   Create a treasure hunt activity with 20 clues for the children to complete in teams on their first night.

7.   Create a code of conduct and reward chart for the children to encourage excellent behaviour and participation.

HINTS AND TIPS 2.3

A LIBRARY OF DRAFTS

Once you have drafts of all these items, you can check, tweak, adjust and improve them, as well as making sure they fit your style and ethos. It will be a lot quicker than starting with an empty page.

HOW CAN GenAI HELP US RAISE THE BAR FOR STUDENT ACHIEVEMENT?

Finally, let's consider the role of GenAI in how we work specifically on raising standards of student achievement. This workflow is a bread-and-butter part of so many teachers' working lives, and teachers using GenAI as a support have the potential to make it faster and more impactful. Let's look at how in Table 2.1.

Table 2.1   Student achievement workflow

Stage	What can GenAI contribute?	What are the benefits?
Assessment	Secure question banks	Low- and high-stakes assessment opportunities
	Personalised and adaptive tests	
	Self-marking tests	
		Data-rich student progress information
Feedback	Personalised feedback	Bias reduction
	Strengths and areas for improvement	Mapping onto rubrics or grade boundaries
Data analysis	Metrics, patterns and trends	Consistent insights and inputs for teacher decisions and support
	Gap analysis	

Stage	What can GenAI contribute?	What are the benefits?
Insights	Predictive models to anticipate future support needs Compare impact of different interventions over time	Well-informed, agile curriculum and lesson-planning decisions Data-rich and insight-led classrooms
Interventions	Tailored recommendations based on outcomes with clear pathway to follow-up	Students get a highly personalised and meaningful experience Parents and teachers have high-quality information

At no point are we replacing the work of the teacher here. This is about augmenting it and amplifying its impact, while boosting the responsibility of students to be active in their own learning journeys.

NOTE IT DOWN

- WHAT DOES SUCCESSFUL LEARNING LOOK LIKE IN AN AI-INFUSED LESSON?

- THINKING YOURSELF INTO THE FUTURE, IMAGINE YOU ARE AN OBSERVER IN ONE OF YOUR OWN LESSONS, WATCHING YOURSELF TEACH A CLASS. DON'T BE TEMPTED TO GET TOO CAUGHT UP IN A SCI-FI FANTASY: LET'S KEEP THIS GROUNDED IN THE POSSIBLE.

- HOW IS GENAI HELPING YOU WITH ...?

- PLANNING

- RESOURCE CREATION

- MARKING

- ASSESSMENT

- DATA AND INSIGHTS

CHAPTER 3
HOW CAN GENERATIVE AI SUPPORT PUPILS WITH SEND?

This chapter covers:

- The benefits of Generative AI for addressing the diverse needs and preferences of pupils with SEND
- How Generative AI can help with inclusion, personalisation, accessibility and adaptive teaching
- How Generative AI can help teachers to adapt teaching and learning to learners' levels, interests and goals, and provide them with individualised feedback and guidance

HOW DOES GenAI HELP TEACHERS WITH INCLUSION FOR PUPILS WITH SEND?

Inclusion is about ensuring equal access to education and providing the necessary support for all students to participate *fully* in their learning environment. It involves adapting the curriculum, teaching methods and learning environments to meet the needs of all learners (InclusiveTeach, 2023). The goal is to create a more equitable and non-discriminatory educational system that recognises and values diversity among students (Schuelka, 2018).

Students' needs in the UK are grouped into four broad categories:

1.   Communication and interaction needs.

2.   Cognition and learning difficulties.

3.   Social, emotional, and mental health difficulties.

4.   Sensory and physical needs.

Table 3.1 gives you a sense of how different types of AI tools can support students with various SEND categories in their learning journey. Notice that GenAI is just part of that story.

Table 3.1   Support for SEND students

SEND Category	Assistive AI	Adaptive AI	Generative AI
Communication and interaction needs	AI-powered speech recognition tools for non-verbal communication	Language learning apps that adapt to individual's pace	Personalised learning materials for social interaction, e.g. symbol-based communication apps

SEND Category	Assistive AI	Adaptive AI	Generative AI
Cognition and learning difficulties	Word prediction software for students with dyslexia	AI-based virtual tutors	Customised educational games and activities, e.g. customised AI-based flashcards and quizzing apps
Social, emotional and mental health difficulties	AI chatbots for social interaction and emotional support	AI therapy tools for mental health support	Responsive journals, CBT-style chatbots, scenarios and simulations for coping strategies, e.g. Reflectly
Sensory and physical needs	Screen readers and voice assistants for visually impaired students	Personalised exercise routines for students with physical disabilities	Tactile learning materials or adaptations for sensory needs, e.g. Microsoft's Seeing AI, which creates audio descriptions of the visual world

In each category, we can use assistive, adaptive and Generative AI technologies to support learning. Sometimes these tools can be combined, or GenAI can provide additional functionality to existing tech.

One thing is clear: we need a *repertoire* of effective practices we can draw upon with agility and ease to reach all of our students and ensure they flourish in their learning.

 HINTS AND TIPS 3.1

GOOD TEACHING FOR ALL

Excellent practice for pupils with SEND is good for everyone in the class.

I particularly like the Universal Design for Learning framework as a starting point for proactive thought about this. This framework helps us think about providing multiple and appropriate means of engagement, representation, action and expression in our lessons. Generative AI can bolster our existing strategies for meeting these needs, and expand our playbook considerably. Let's explore how.

LITERACY IS KEY

Fundamentally, students need core literacy skills to *access* the curriculum. From phonics and vocabulary to fluency and comprehension, literacy is fundamental for learning. SEND can so often be a barrier to literacy for learning, and GenAI is a powerful tool for supporting teachers with a range of strategies to meet their students' needs in this area.

Strategies to explore:

1. **Dual coding:** Reduce cognitive load and lower demands on working memory by presenting information both verbally and visually. Use GenAI to create helpful imagery to support comprehension and retention.

2. **Summarising:** Identify key information, organise ideas, focus in on the main concepts and model analytical processes. Use GenAI to create summaries of longer texts to help engage with and navigate complex texts and extract the most valuable information.

3. **Reading assistants and coaches:** Build confidence, provide immediate personalised feedback, give real-time corrections and improve fluency. Use GenAI to tailor the experience, engage reluctant readers with co-creation, and target challenging words with additional practice.

4. **Multimodal reading (also ear reading):** Provide an auditory approach in parallel to the visual one using audiobooks, text-to speech, or accessibility tools. Use GenAI to customise reading content, build fluency, grow confidence with new material, give real-time definitions and allow access to content that might otherwise be out of reach.

5. **Live translation for EAL learners:** Give students access to live translation tools to allow them to understand teacher inputs, engage in dialogue, access and infer meaning and demonstrate comprehension. Use GenAI to provide real-time translation, live presentations, support paired or group work and provide interpreting inputs for parent–teacher consultations.

6. **Levelling reading passages:** Create multiple versions of core texts according to the reading levels of learners in the class, making content accessible and comprehensible, and ensuring that the curriculum content is delivered in an inclusive way. Use GenAI to adjust and align the reading level of a text, add vocabulary lists and glossaries and tailor the content to the needs of the students with multiple versions as needed.

7. **Chunking curriculum content:** Break down complex inputs into smaller, more manageable parts to support understanding, especially of processes, timelines, connected ideas and the relative influence of different factors. Use GenAI to divide content, create headers and build a logical sequence and pace of the learning materials.

 REFLECTION 3.1

Which of these strategies would most benefit your students? Select three you would like to try.

1.

2.

3.

HOW CAN GenAI HELP TEACHERS PROVIDE ADAPTIVE TEACHING FOR PUPILS WITH SEND?

Now let's zoom out from literacy to look at other ways that GenAI can help us provide additional support for our learners with SEND. There is much teacher time to be saved here and, of course, there are many opportunities to leverage technology to help your students with their learning.

HINTS AND TIPS 3.2

SEND IS CORE

Remember, additional support for learning with SEND is not a 'nice to have' extra, but a core part of what it means to do our job.

The Initial Teacher Training and Early Career Framework makes it clear that teachers should 'learn that technology, including educational software and assistive technology, can support teaching and learning for pupils with SEND' and should learn how to 'provide opportunities for all pupils to experience success by ... making effective and judicious use of specialist technology' (gov.uk, 2024).

SCAFFOLDING LEARNING

This is a strategic and temporary form of support that enables pupils with SEND to achieve learning tasks that they might not be able to start or complete independently. As the student gains independence, mastery and confidence, you can gradually reduce the support. What might this look like?

IDEAS FOR THE CLASSROOM 3.1

- **Writing frames:** Create a writing frame to support Year 8 students as they complete their own explanation of the photosynthesis process, including sections for sunlight, water, carbon dioxide and glucose, with the result being 150 words long. Add a glossary of key terms underneath.

- **Partially completed texts/cloze activities:** Write a cloze exercise paragraph describing the photosynthesis process, leaving ten blank spaces on key nouns and verbs.

- **Model answers:** Provide a 70–100-word model answer for the question: 'Explain how plants convert light energy into chemical energy during photosynthesis'.

- **Knowledge organisers:** Outline 20 elements that a teacher would need to create a knowledge organiser for the key terms and concepts related to photosynthesis for a Year 9 student.

- **Planning and reflection prompts:** Create five simple reflective prompts to support students through planning and undergoing an experiment to test the effects of light intensity on the rate of photosynthesis.

- **Sentence starters:** Generate ten sentence starters to help students begin their responses to an essay question about the importance of photosynthesis in ecosystems.

Remember, you can add specifics about the learning needs, answer keys, reading ages, language and parameters for your prompts here, so do experiment with it and see what you can create.

 RESOURCES 3.1

There are many GenAI tools and platforms that you can use to develop resources for scaffolding learning. Two that I particularly recommend are diffit.me and teachmateai.com. Both are accessible for free. Go and give them a try.

ORGANISATION, ROUTINES AND RESILIENCE

Alongside the cognitive processes of learning, we know that there are many ways non-cognitive skills can support learners with SEND in their work. In some cases, teachers can provide materials and inputs and, in others, we can give the student access to GenAI-powered tools. In many cases here, GenAI adds a layer of additional functionality on top of existing tech solutions. This is a space in which it shows great promise for the future, so keep an eye open for what comes next!

SELF-MANAGEMENT

- Goal-setting
- Prioritising
- Self-advocacy and agency
- Independence
- Organisation

MOTIVATION AND ENGAGEMENT

- Fine-tuning feedback
- Developing growth mindset
- Tailoring experiences to match special interests
- Gamifying challenges to promote resilience

PERSONALISATION: INDIVIDUALISED INSTRUCTION

There is evidence that digital tools used to provide individualised instruction can have a positive impact on student progress. The practical limitations of doing this by traditional methods mean that, of course, we can't provide a personal tutor for every child in school. However, GenAI tools have an important role to play in supporting teaching, by creating a personalised tutor-coach experience which promotes progress on a 1–1 basis. We can train Large Language Models to deploy mastery techniques, Socratic questioning, public examination rubrics, metacognitive strategies to boost retention ... and many more tools that teachers use.

One example of this is the creation of learning platforms with personalised curriculum pathways, where learning goals, concept understanding and existing knowledge create a journey through a map of learning materials and assessments that match the individual's needs. This type of system often combines machine learning and GenAI, allowing the system to track progress and then respond according to assessment along the way. I predict we will see more of these tools soon; they are designed as a supplement to teacher support in class.

NOTE IT DOWN

Write down three ways you would like to explore using GenAI to support adaptive teaching. What benefits do you hope these strategies will bring to your lessons? How will you know if they are effective for your students?

CHAPTER 4
HOW CAN GENERATIVE AI INSPIRE CREATIVITY AND INNOVATION?

This chapter covers:

- Stimulating creativity, experimentation and innovation
- Creating novel and diverse content to support the learning process
- Practical suggestions for using Generative AI to spark creativity in your lesson planning

STIMULATING CREATIVITY, EXPERIMENTATION AND INNOVATION

This chapter is going to give you a sense of how GenAI can get your creative juices flowing when it comes to teaching and learning, resource and content creation and planning. We know how important it is to keep our professional practice fresh, and there is no doubt that stoking the fire of creativity, experimentation and innovation will support great learning in our classrooms.

At no point would I suggest that teachers cannot be stunningly creative in their own right; there is evidence to the contrary in classrooms up and down the country. However, sometimes we hit the limits of our imaginations, experience, stamina and time; I think GenAI can provide meaningful and exciting supplementary inputs that should not be ignored. As teachers, it is our mission to build a compelling and effective learning journey for our students that engages, challenges and supports them as they travel through it. It's also important that our work ignites our own imaginations and inspires us too. Let's explore how GenAI can help us do that.

AUGMENTED IDEATION

First, let's explore the concept of 'augmented ideation', where GenAI assists in idea generation. Teachers spend a lot of time and energy coming up with approaches for achieving a desired outcome, solving problems and making plans. We can use GenAI as part of that creative process, and leverage tools to help us augment our own creativity.

KICKSTARTING CREATIVITY AND GETTING 'UNSTUCK'

Sometimes, getting ideas flowing is tough. Perhaps the blank page is triggering writer's block, we are anxious about getting things wrong, or not having good ideas. We can alleviate some of those obstacles and remove the fear of the blank page by using GenAI to *scaffold idea generation* with structured approaches such as mind mapping, or story starters. We can take a playful, expansive, or boundary-pushing approach to the prompts we use when opening our thinking to unconventional or novel ideas, giving us a sense of freedom and choice about which ones we choose to explore further. It also helps when perhaps our self-esteem tells us we can't possibly do something, but GenAI bolsters us by aligning with our thoughts and validating what we were uncertain about, in a process we could call 'co-creativity'. There are clearly going to be some ethical aspects to consider here, which we will unpack later in Chapter 5.

CREATING ORIGINAL MATERIAL

GenAI can aid in creating original content, such as writing, music, video, images, code, or art. There is a huge explosion of new platforms and tools being launched in this space, such as Open AI's Jukebox which is a tool for making music. Searching for recommendations online will yield some fun and interesting opportunities for experimentation, but explore with care to ensure you choose platforms that work ethically with creators.

I think this is a really useful way to explore expression, boost creative output and bring into the world ideas and experiences in ways that lack of skill might previously have prevented. This is contentious stuff, as we will explore later in this chapter, but I think we miss a trick as teachers if we do not bring the best of our selves and the technology available to us to the job we do.

VISUALISING, ORGANISING AND EXPLORING IDEAS

We know that providing illustrations and visual inputs alongside text can help with cognitive load in learning. Why not try creating imagery to bring your resources, documents and slides to life? Using GenAI to produce concept illustrations to bridge the gap between the abstract and the tangible and help promote understanding and creative response. We can also use visualisations to explore data, algorithms, processes, workflows and cause/effect.

> I find it particularly helpful to be able to gather
> a messy or chaotic list of my ideas together and use
> GenAI to help me find a sense of order and hierarchy.
> I have even done that as part of the process of writing
> this chapter. Let's remember too, that these techniques
> will be just as helpful for students when prototyping
> and testing their innovative ideas too.

PROVOCATIONS, DEBATE AND CHALLENGING CONVENTIONS

Lively debate and engaging discussions can stimulate extensive thinking and intellectual growth. GenAI can help us by generating thought-provoking stimuli which can encourage reflection, critical thinking and the consideration of broader viewpoints outside our own and our students' lived experience.

HINTS AND TIPS 4.1

ROLEPLAYS OR SCENES

I have found GenAI especially helpful when creating roleplays or scenes for students to explore a context in depth.

It also allows us to depersonalise, translate, or neutralise situations that may be sensitive to make them more accessible and engaging.

IDEAS FOR THE CLASSROOM 4.1

Why not try developing examples, scenarios and scripts for your classes that help you step out of the predictable and allow for some free-range reflection, especially if it allows you to celebrate high-level thinking and interdisciplinary connections.

ITERATING AND REFINING IDEAS

If we look to design thinking approaches, we know that the skills of iteration and refinement are key for success. Often, we can get to a faster and higher-quality outcome via trial and error than if we take a one-and-done approach, especially if at each stage we can learn from feedback and adaptation. This honing, crafting and experimentation can help us neutralise risk aversion and perfectionism and can help us step beyond the boundaries of our pre-existing skills or knowledge. You can use GenAI to help you explore, experiment and extrapolate your ideas too.

REFLECTION 4.1

What kinds of creative skills would you like to foster in your teaching practice?

What can GenAI do to help you amplify these to produce high-quality outcomes?

CREATING NOVEL AND DIVERSE CONTENT TO SUPPORT THE LEARNING PROCESS

Now, let us explore how GenAI can assist us through creating content to support the learning process.

METACOGNITION

GenAI can act in a coach-like manner, helping us to reflect actively on our processes and results, to improve our self-awareness, manage our tasks proactively and develop agency in how we control our workflow (Dellarocas, 2023).

 IDEAS FOR THE CLASSROOM 4.2

- Use GenAI to model a specific process such as essay planning, and then create scaffolds for students to interrogate their own strategies for effectiveness.

- Use GenAI to create prompts for reflective journal entries for your students to consider their process, strategies, knowledge and outcomes in alignment with your specific goals.

- Use GenAI to develop a roleplaying scenario where students have to defend an argument, explain a concept, or justify a decision in ways that highlight the metacognitive reasoning you want to develop.

- Use GenAI to develop peer review models and frameworks to support students in becoming more reflective and in developing their critical thinking.

CREATING CONNECTIONS

Identifying gaps and targeting specific areas with tailored learning resources: adaptive questioning, for example.

'We all know that developing rich, connected schemas in the minds of our children is a sure-fire way to be able to create, develop and embed knowledge. Once one branch of a schema has been forged, it acts as arm [sic] which reaches out as a hook to welcome new knowledge' (Fayaz, 2021).

The interconnectedness of ideas and understanding can be contextualised within comparative and contrasting aspects of individual topics. How things fit together is part of creating schema.

IDEAS FOR THE CLASSROOM 4.3

- Use GenAI to pose Socratic questions that support deeper thinking and prompt connections with other themes or topics.

- Use GenAI to help you create concept maps that allow you to link ideas and concepts together.

- Use GenAI to develop scenarios that allow hypothetical exploration of ideas and transfer knowledge into new domains.

- Use GenAI to provide multiple solutions or perspectives on a problem or decision, and then support students in thinking critically about the options.

BROADENING AND DIVERSIFYING THE CURRICULUM

GenAI, when prompted to do so, can provide us with positive opportunities as teachers to add diverse content, examples and narratives into the curriculum. However, we cannot take it for granted that this will happen automatically. Just like in analogue human society, bias and habits are 'baked in' to GenAI via the material it was originally trained with, so we need to prompt specifically for diversity. We can hope that the more we do this, the more the large language models will adapt.

 IDEAS FOR THE CLASSROOM 4.4

- Ask GenAI to analyse and review existing content for bias, and provide suggestions or additions for more balanced or varied viewpoints.

- Ask GenAI to provide research inputs from underrepresented groups in the fields of study you are exploring, and ensure that examples or case studies come from a geographic, socio-economic, cultural, linguistic, religious, or ethic range of examples.

- Use GenAI to create scenarios, discussion questions, or models that involve characters and settings from diverse backgrounds, and ensure that the narrative is respectful, culturally accurate and meaningful.

- Use GenAI to support translations or adaptations of content from different languages, dialects or regional variations to boost linguistic openness.

PRACTICAL SUGGESTIONS FOR USING GENERATIVE AI TO SPARK CREATIVITY IN YOUR LESSON PLANNING

Let's think now about how we might use GenAI to help us with engaging our students, planning interesting lessons and developing effective ways to learn new content.

GEOGRAPHY

Suggested prompt: *Design an assessed task for Year 7 Geography students to find out how well they have understood and retained the core concepts and specialist language they have learned about the topic of rivers, including the water cycle, the movement of water, the journey of the river, meanders and waterfalls. Include a fun, creative activity to demonstrate their learning that will be engaging and challenging. Add a simple rubric and scoring system with an answer key and success criteria.*

OUTPUT (AI GENERATED RESPONSE)

Assessed Task – The Great River Escape

Objective: To assess Year 7 students' understanding of rivers in a fun and engaging way, incorporating the water cycle, river movement, meanders, and waterfalls.

Task Description: Students will create a comic strip titled "The Great River Escape," where water droplets embark on an epic adventure from the river's source to the sea, encountering various geographical features along the way.

Instructions:

1. **Character Creation:** Design your water droplet characters with unique personalities.

2. **Comic Strip Planning:** Sketch a storyboard for your comic strip, outlining the key stages of the water cycle and river journey.

3. **Illustration and Dialogue:** Draw your comic strip, ensuring to include speech bubbles that explain each stage and feature.

4. **Humour and Creativity:** Inject humour into your story. Maybe the water droplets are on a secret mission or must navigate through 'dangerous' meanders.

5. **Presentation:** Share your comic strip with the class and explain the geographical concepts depicted.

Rubric and Scoring System:

- **Creativity and Humour (20 points):** Original and humorous depiction of the river's journey.

- **Geographical Accuracy (50 points):** Correct representation of the water cycle and river features.

- **Artistic Expression (20 points):** Quality of illustrations and character design.

- **Explanation and Engagement (10 points):** Ability to explain the comic strip and engage the audience.

Total Points: 100

Success Criteria:

- The comic strip must include all stages of the water cycle and river journey.

- Key river features such as meanders and waterfalls are creatively integrated.

- Dialogue within speech bubbles demonstrates understanding of the concepts.

- The presentation is entertaining and educational.

Answer Key:

- **Water Cycle:** Evaporation, condensation, precipitation, collection.

- **River Journey:** Source, upper course, middle course, lower course, mouth.

Glossary:

- **Evaporation:** The process of turning from liquid into vapor.

- **Condensation:** Water that collects as droplets on a cold surface when humid air is in contact with it.

- **Precipitation:** Rain, snow, sleet, or hail that falls to the ground.

- **Meander:** A winding curve or bend in a river.

- **Waterfall:** A cascade of water falling from a height, formed when a river or stream flows over a precipice or steep incline.

COMPUTER SCIENCE

Suggested prompt: *Create a light-hearted paired debugging activity for Year 9 students working on Python using print statements, if, else, elif statements, inputs and f strings. Include five errors for the students to find, and one more challenging task (which could be more structural). Provide clear instructions, a funny scenario and stimulus questions the students could ask each other to methodically approach their debugging activity. Add a glossary at the end of key terms and code snippets to support the learners.*

OUTPUT (AI GENERATED RESPONSE):

Activity: The Case of the Python Pizza Party

Scenario: You are the proud owner of the Python Pizzeria, where the pizzas are coded to perfection. However, your latest Python script for taking orders has gone haywire. It's giving out pizzas that nobody ordered. Your mission is to debug the script before the hungry hordes of Year 9 students arrive for the pizza party.

Instructions: Work in pairs to find and fix the errors in the script. There are five obvious mistakes and one more challenging structural issue. Use the questions provided to guide your debugging process.

Python Script with Errors:

```python
# Welcome to Python Pizzeria!
def order_pizza():
    print("Welcome to Python Pizzeria!")
    pizza_flavour = input("What flavor of
pizza would you like? ")

    if pizza_flavor == "Pepperoni":
        print(f"Great choice! One {pizza_
flavour} pizza coming right up!")
    elif pizza_flavor = "Cheese":
        print(f"Yum! A {pizza_flavour} pizza
will be with you shortly!")
    else
        print("Sorry, we don't have that
flavor. How about a Mystery Pizza?")
    pizza_size = input("What size pizza
would you like? (S, M, L) ")
    if pizza_size == "S":
        prize = 5
    elif pizza_size == "M":
        price == 7
    elif pizza_size == "L":
        price = 10
    else:
        print("We only have S, M, L sizes.
Defaulting to Medium".)
        price = 7

    print(f"Your order: {pizza_flavour}
pizza, size {pizza_size}. Total: {price}")

order_pizza()
```

Stimulus Questions:

• "What error message are we getting, and which line does it point to?"

- "Are there any typos in variable names or syntax errors we can spot?"

- "Is the program using the correct comparison operators?"

- "Are all the branches of the if/else statements properly closed?"

- "Does the f-string syntax look correct, and are we using the right variables within it?"

Glossary:

- **print**: A function that outputs text to the console.

- **input**: A function that reads text input from the user.

- **if, elif, else**: Conditional statements that execute different blocks of code based on certain conditions.

- **f-string**: A string formatting mechanism in Python that allows for embedding expressions inside string literals, using curly braces {}.

- **variable**: A name that refers to a value stored in the program's memory.

Challenge Task: The structural issue lies in the logic of the pizza size pricing. Can you refactor the code to handle the pizza size and price in a more efficient way?

Happy debugging and, remember, every bug you squash brings you closer to a delicious slice of victory!

HISTORY

Suggested prompt: *Create a Year 6 History lesson to celebrate Black History Month on the theme of peace. Build in examples of Black creators, writers, poets, musicians etc., whose work the children can explore on this theme.*

Ensure the content is age-appropriate for 10–11-year-olds, it includes opportunities for reflection and creativity, and aligns with the school's goals of developing cultural literacy, openness and anti-racism.

OUTPUT (AI GENERATED RESPONSE):

Year 6 History Lesson Plan: Celebrating Peace in Black History

Objective: To explore the theme of peace through the work of Black creators, writers, poets, and musicians, fostering cultural literacy, openness, and anti-racism among Year 6 students.

Introduction (10 minutes): Begin with a class discussion on what peace means to the students. Introduce Black History Month and explain its significance.

Exploration of Black Creators (20 minutes):

- *Jorja Smith: Listen to her music and discuss the peaceful messages conveyed through her lyrics.*

- *Momtaza Mehri: Read excerpts from her poetry, focusing on themes of peace and unity.*

- *George the Poet: Analyse his spoken word pieces that promote social harmony.*

- *Benjamin Zephaniah: Explore his poems that advocate for racial equality and peace.*

Activity – Peace Poetry (20 minutes): Students will write their own short poems or songs inspired by the creators discussed. Encourage them to express what peace means to them and how it can be achieved in their communities.

Reflection and Sharing (15 minutes): Students share their poems with the class. Discuss how these works contribute to understanding and promoting peace.

Conclusion (10 minutes): Wrap up by reflecting on how the works of Black creators can inspire peace and understanding. Discuss how students can apply these lessons in their daily lives.

Homework: Assign students to research another Black creator, writer, poet, or musician whose work embodies the theme of peace and prepare a short presentation for the next class.

This lesson plan is designed to be engaging and age-appropriate, encouraging students to think critically about the theme of peace and how it is expressed in the creative works of Black individuals.

NOTE IT DOWN

WHICH ASPECTS OF YOUR PLANNING AND LESSON DELIVERY COULD BENEFIT MOST FROM THE SUPPORT OF GENERATIVE AI AND ITS CREATIVE POTENTIAL? HOW WILL YOU EXPERIMENT WITH THIS NEXT?

CHAPTER 5

WHAT ARE THE CHALLENGES AND RISKS WITH USING GENERATIVE AI IN EDUCATION?

This chapter covers:

- The inherent difficulties and limitations of Generative AI technology
- Plagiarism and ethical use
- Accuracy and hallucination
- AI and safeguarding

UNDERSTANDING DIFFICULTIES AND LIMITATIONS

Understanding the inherent difficulties and limitations of Generative AI technology, and the pitfalls and concerns we need to avoid, is an important part of learning to use the tools well in our professional practice. This will help us make good decisions, choose the best tool for the task we want to achieve and ensure that the output we create is of high quality. It will also help us judge when the right time is to use GenAI, and when we might be better off choosing another approach.

PLAGIARISM

One of the main concerns many teachers share is around plagiarism and ethical use. It makes complete sense: so much of the work we do with students in terms of assessment and feedback relies on a strong foundation of integrity. In years gone by, there was a very clear divide between a student's own work and something which was copied from a friend, lifted (without acknowledgement) from a book or a webpage, or which was written by someone else on their behalf.

That simple clarity has been lost, and the dividing line between 'your own work' and 'someone else's work' is fuzzier than it was. This is partly because of the co-creational process which happens when we use GenAI and partly because of the challenges around how to acknowledge the content produced in the moment by a large language model rather than a person. As adults, we understand that what matters here is integrity: presenting ideas from another source or person *as your own* is not acceptable.

 REFLECTION 5.1

How can we help our students understand the importance of integrity here? What is best practice?

GenAI is new, and we do not yet have established and accepted norms for how to reference and acknowledge it in our writing. Academic authors are increasingly providing guidance on these which steers away from listing GenAI tools as 'authors' or 'co-authors', and instead disclosing the use of GenAI in methodology or acknowledgements, with information about the name and version of the tool used, the date accessed and the URL (Player, 2024).

 IDEAS FOR THE CLASSROOM 5.1

For school students, citing GenAI where it is appropriate feels like an important step towards transparency and integrity.

There is not yet clear academic consistency about how best to cite or acknowledge GenAI in academic work in this way, but including details of the name and version of the system used – for example, ChatGPT-3.5; the company that made the AI system – for example, OpenAI; the URL of the AI system; and a single sentence describing the context and date(s) in which the tool was used seems a functional approach where no further guidance is available. For example: 'I acknowledge the use of Microsoft Copilot https://copilot.microsoft.com/ during March 2024 for research and summarisation purposes, and to proofread my initial draft.'

Of course, in some contexts it is completely inappropriate to use GenAI at all. At the time of writing, JCQ and UCAS have made it very clear that GenAI has no place in the creation of personal statements or coursework. What matters most is that we teach students how to acknowledge and reference their sources effectively and instil a really clear understanding of expectations around plagiarism.

ACCURACY AND HALLUCINATION

Generative AI can unintentionally produce responses that *look* plausible, but in fact are not accurate. Confusing fact with fiction, misrepresenting information, filling in gaps with inaccurate statistics and even generating surreal or nonsensical outputs; these sorts of errors are relatively common. These are known as *hallucinations* and are one of the downsides of this technology. Let's be clear: GenAI does not *think*, *understand,* or *know* **anything**, and is blind to values.

GitHub's hallucination leaderboard shows that even the best GenAI models hallucinate about 3 per cent of the time, and many others are hallucinating between 4 and 12 per cent of the time. That's a lot (search Github Hallucination Leaderboard to find the latest figures on this).

 # HINTS AND TIPS 5.1

EVALUATION

How do I evaluate AI-generated material? When considering AI-generated material, it's useful to look at it through these eight lenses to support iteration and improvement.

Table 5.1   The eight lenses for AI evaluation

	High	Low
Value	Insightful	Not relevant
	Thought-provoking	Lacks substance
	Useful and correct	'Waffly' or wrong
Breadth	Covers or considers diverse topics or perspectives	Focuses on a single niche
Depth	Thorough exploration of concept	Surface-level or simplistic exploration
'Groundedness'	Based on fact, empirical evidence, logical reasoning	Lacks any factual basis, relies on assumptions or weak sources of evidence
Uniqueness	Offers novel viewpoints, fresh perspectives, or creative elements	Repetitive, bland, cliched, or lacking originality
Coherence	Ideas flow logically and consistently together, with appropriate cause–effect connections	Incoherent assumptions, connections, or poor flow makes for a lack of a cohesive structure

	High	Low
Adaptability	Can be repurposed or modified for multiple contexts	Highly tailored and specific to a single context
Appeal	Visually or verbally appealing through design elements, humour, aesthetics, etc.	Lacks appeal and is not engaging

How can we avoid falling foul of hallucinations? It's not a realistic goal to double-check all content produced by GenAI, but we should expect to sense-check the responses to our prompts where we are beyond the scope of our own expertise and common sense. Triangulating new information with reliable sources is part of taking responsibility for how we use GenAI and will help us avoid misinformation or inaccuracy in our work. Where our instincts ring alarm bells, we should listen!

 HINTS AND TIPS 5.2

SENSE CHECKING

- **Redrafting and reiterating prompts to triangulate outputs.**

- **Critical thinking and asking exploratory questions.**

- **Recognising bias and challenging it proactively.**

- **Fact checking and rigorous accountability in research.**

- **Perspective-taking and developing agility with viewpoints.**

INTELLECTUAL OFFLOADING AND BLIND RELIANCE

This is the practice of using GenAI tools to reduce the cognitive demands of a task. Taking shortcuts like this might speed up the process and free up the student to engage in deeper thought, but it may also undermine their conceptual understanding, critical thinking, recall and intellectual stamina. Some academics are concerned about 'cognitive enfeeblement' and 'capability decay' as a result. Deep learning involves engagement, not shortcuts.

The human brain is capable of wonderful, unexpected ideas and connections, and we should make sure that we are clear in our own minds where the uncrossable lines should be. For us to outsource our creativity would be to lose something that is inherently and brilliantly human and replace it with something that cannot necessarily capture the essence of lived experience, human insight, or hard-earned skill. I would not go as far as to argue that we owe it to our students to pour our hearts and souls into every worksheet we create, but the business of teaching is inherently relational; if we offload the responsibility for our ideas, we risk losing our depth of connection with their meaning too. The demise of human creativity and academic integrity is well covered in academic research, and something teachers will need to work proactively to avoid.

Part of the process of building integrity and trustworthiness into our teaching and task design must be reconsidering both the process and the product of the work we are asking students to complete. Witnessing the learning, thinking, planning and problem-solving processes as part of the journey to the result will help us ensure the integrity and authenticity of the whole learning journey, rather than just the final flourish. We will explore task design further in Chapter 6.

SAFEGUARDING AND WELLBEING

Above all else, our responsibility towards the children we work with centres around keeping them safe.

When considering the potential risks of GenAI usage in school, there are some key areas to be aware of. This will depend on the extent to which the tools are being used by staff or students or both.

1. **Inappropriate content:** It is not possible to pre-screen every prompt result, and GenAI can product content that is explicit or inappropriate. This may include issues relating to protected characteristics.

2. **Bullying and harassment:** GenAI can be used as a tool to generate harmful, hurtful, or hateful content, or can be used as an aggravating factor in existing bullying scenarios to amplify the damage inflicted by harmful behaviour.

3. **Impersonation, extortion and predatory behaviours:** Predators and GenAI-created content can be used to manipulate or exploit unsuspecting or vulnerable youngsters by simulating human-like appearances or interactions, and duping them into acting in ways that may be inappropriate or harmful.

4. **Synthetic intimacy:** Unscrupulous creators may prey upon the vulnerable, the naive, the lonely and the inexperienced via platforms designed to use GenAI to create the illusion of friendship, romance, attraction, or a confidante.

BIAS

AI models, like humans, have bias 'baked in' to them.

The data that AI models were trained on came from human outputs like social media posts, news articles and blogs. This means that GenAI's responses can be skewed or misleading as a result of this built-in bias. We should think critically about bias and AI and examine our outputs through a variety of lenses depending on the context, including language, gender, race and ethnicity, age, disability, geographical location, socio-economic factors and legal frameworks. Recent research is well worth exploring in this space, especially on gender and ethnicity. Without users taking proactive measures to challenge bias in our prompts and choice of tools, we risk presenting learners with a worldview that is skewed at best, and oppressive and discriminatory at worst.

 REFLECTION 5.2

What biases do you have that you need to be actively aware of? What do you need to do to recognise them and mitigate them?

DATA AND PRIVACY

There is controversy in the world of GenAI as just in the way it exists, arguably, it has the potential to violate GDPR in a number of ways, including the right to be forgotten and the right to consent to having data extracted or saved, purpose limitation, intellectual property and data subject rights. Regulatory bodies are having to play catch-up as this landscape shifts.

DIGITAL GAPS WIDENING

GenAI typically requires access to the latest technology, fast internet connections and, often, high-quality tools are behind a paid subscription. We know from the social media model that there is no such thing as a free tool: if you are not paying for it, then you, your data and your attention are the product. All this leads us to be concerned that GenAI may cause digital gaps to widen for young people; there is work to be done to counteract this. Check out the work of the Good Future Foundation, a UK-based non-profit organisation aiming to do just that!

In this chapter, we have explored some key challenges connected to GenAI in education, including plagiarism, accuracy and hallucination, intellectual offloading and unhealthy reliance on AI. We also considered some of the risks we face when using these tools – principally, safeguarding concerns, bias, data and privacy being compromised and the widening of digital gaps. The next chapter will provide some insights into the best approaches to combat these concerns.

NOTE IT DOWN

- WHAT ARE YOU MOST CONCERNED ABOUT WHEN
  CONSIDERING THE USE OF GENERATIVE AI IN SCHOOLS?

- WHAT DO YOU NEED TO KNOW MORE ABOUT?

CHAPTER 6
USING GENERATIVE AI RESPONSIBLY IN SCHOOLS

This chapter covers:

- Recommendations for using Generative AI responsibly, effectively and safely in the classroom
- How we can approach boundaries, task design and AI detection
- How to approach pupils' use of AI tools and develop AI literacy
- How we can prepare students to flourish in an AI-infused world

MOVING FORWARDS WITH RESPONSIBLE USE OF AI

The first thing that happens when humans are faced with an innovation they do not fully understand and cannot fully control is an instinctive desire to put a blanket ban on it, block it, or remove it. This is a waste of time (that horse has already bolted) and a squandered opportunity. Older students will be using GenAI already anyway, and it is far more important for us to teach them to use it well and wisely, than sweep it under the carpet and make it a taboo subject.

Instead, let's consider how we can effectively ensure that AI is used when it is appropriate to do so. This is a cultural question for you, your classroom and your school, and it starts with the expectations that are set and then enforced, about doing the right thing when no one is looking. Never has integrity mattered quite this much when using technology for learning.

As teachers, we should see ourselves as the primary users of AI for learning in that we design, facilitate and safeguard the students' experiences with it. Students will learn from us as role models and teachers, so our own approach is key. By reading this book, you have already shown a brilliant commitment to your professional development, and I hope that you feel that decision is validated by just how important your role will be, moving forwards.

BOUNDARIES, RULES AND RESTRICTIONS

What will the adults do when the *children* misuse GenAI? What will the adults do when *other adults* misuse GenAI? Having clear guidance and policy in place on a school-wide level is a good idea, so that the boundary between doing the right thing and doing the wrong thing is clear, and the consequences are consistent. We want to make it so that 'using GenAI is fine as long as you don't get caught' isn't the default. This clear guidance will need additional detail or more precision when it comes to high-stakes assessment, homework tasks, or preparation for coursework. But let's be clear: when students are unsupervised, we have little recourse to anything other than their conscience or fear of being caught to bolster our authority. There are two ends of a scale here:

OPEN

Open-book, open-browser, open-notes, open-GenAI tools, can collaborate, low or no supervision

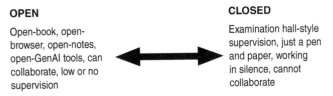

CLOSED

Examination hall-style supervision, just a pen and paper, working in silence, cannot collaborate

Figure 6.1   The two ends of the GenAI scale

You will need to make conscious choices about task design and access to resources, in order to make sure that your tasks' utility is not eroded. We know that finding the right challenge level at both ends of the spectrum is tricky, but as GenAI tools get more sophisticated, task setting at the open end gets more complex.

 HINTS AND TIPS 6.1

PROCESS AND OUTCOME

At the open end, there should be an emphasis on capturing and assessing the *process* of thinking through the task, whereas, at the closed end, the goal is to review the *outcome* of the thinking.

As you plan work, build tasks and set assignments, consider how you can assess both the process of completion and the outcome. Making transparent the intellectual cogs turning, the connections made, the research completed, the planning of ideas will help you support the personal accountability of the student, the integrity of the task outcomes and the validity of the data it creates.

REFLECTION 6.1

What does this 'process of completion' look like in your subject?

AI DETECTION

Detection apps do not work reliably. Louder for the colleagues at the back: *AI detection apps do not work reliably.* Certainly not reliably enough to base judgements about academic integrity and student outcomes on their outputs. In particular, they discriminate unfairly against EAL students and those using support tools and reference materials for their writing.

What works much better is *knowing your students and their work*. The best AI detection tool is completely free and takes just a few moments. Asking the student questions about their work will quickly show you what you need to know: 'Tell me more about the example you used in this paragraph', or 'Which source did you use for this case study?', or 'Explain this concept to me.' If confused looks or uncomfortable silence are your only reply, you know what has happened.

HINTS AND TIPS 6.2

NO SHORTCUT

There is no shortcut for playing the long game when it comes to integrity in school.

Younger students should experience what it means to be accountable for their decisions at a low-stakes level well before things get more serious as they complete their UCAS applications, job applications, coursework, NEAs — where even a hint of a suspicion of AI misuse will yield catastrophic results.

We should imagine how exhausting and indeed demoralising it will be for students, especially those who are high-performing and conscientious, to be regularly suspected or accused of cheating. Deep empathy for your learners will support your approach and ensure that your classroom culture isn't polluted with unhelpful negativity from suspicion or resentment.

KEEPING CHILDREN SAFE: AGE RESTRICTIONS

Setting ground rules for the use of GenAI among students is important, and the first pillar of those rules should be age-appropriate autonomy. At the time of writing this is a fast-changing space, so I recommend you start with the prevailing international legal requirements, which will include the EU AI Act, COPPA and GDPR, the US legal regulations about AI and the individual platform Ts + Cs. In many cases, students between the ages of 13 and 18 will need parental consent, and those under 13 should only be using GenAI on platforms specifically created for that age-group with the appropriate consents, supervision and safeguards in place.

Unfortunately, the social media machine stole a march on regulation and attitudes, which has meant many young people are blasé about age limits and restrictions, and families can be naive about the risks for children associated with platforms and content designed for adults. Let's make sure those same mistakes are not made with GenAI.

HOW CAN WE PREPARE STUDENTS FOR AN AI-INFUSED WORLD?

We are in the business of human flourishing. We plant the seeds that grow into academic, practical and creative success for our students. In an AI-infused world where technology has changed and will continue to change so many contexts, there are qualities and skills that will help young people become thriving adults. Let's consider them alongside the desirable processes and outcomes that would support excellent lifelong learning.

Table 6.1 Qualities and skills to support learning

Qualities and skills	Processes	Outcomes
Critical thinking	Exercising judgement, evaluation and analysis	Cultural literacy
		Adapting knowledge to new contexts
Curiosity	Questioning, exploring, triangulating ideas	Lifelong learning habits
		Intellectual openness
Intrinsic motivation	Resilience, patience	Achievement and striving
Self-regulation	Conscious choice-making	Adaptability
Self-esteem	Balance of humility and confidence	High-quality decision-making
		Resistance to intellectual offloading
Creativity	Idea generation and development	Solutions, problem-solving, innovation, beauty and entrepreneurship
Character	Moral frameworks, contextual sensitivity	Integrity and ethical understanding
		Personal accountability
Communication and collaboration	Listening effectively, articulating ideas	Healthy relational awareness and teamwork
Digital and AI literacy	Interaction with tools and technologies	High-quality engagement and deployment of tools with context-appropriate deftness

There are lots of these aspects that already exist in our schools and curricula, but to develop and nurture them we will need to create explicit opportunities for modelling, learning and development. The aims to hold on to are threefold: we want our students to be responsible users of AI, active co-creators of AI and the future leaders of design and development of the next generations of AI.

While we are taking a positive and optimistic approach to this, there is a darker side to the future of AI we should also guard against. Young people are growing up in a society where manipulation of the media and the concept of truth makes understanding what is really happening in the world challenging. Deep fakes, harassment, misinformation and manipulation, fake news, synthetic intimacy and extortion are all AI-fuelled issues that may cross the desk of your pastoral leads in the near future if they have not already.

 REFLECTION 6.2

Which of these areas is your first priority for your students? How could you adapt your existing planning to make future-focused skills more prominent?

AI COMPETENCIES AND AI LITERACY

Having considered the wider educational framework for developing learners who will thrive in an AI-infused world, let's now zoom in to focus on specific competencies for students to enable them to be skilled users of this technology.

As part of its broader 'Artificial Intelligence and the Futures of Learning' (UNESCO, 2023) initiative, UNESCO is developing competency frameworks for teachers and students. There are (at the time of writing) four strands: human-centred mindset, ethics of AI, AI techniques and applications, and AI system design. Do search online to find out more about this, and use these frameworks to support your curriculum thinking, as well as your professional development.

NOTE IT DOWN

WE DON'T NEED TO START FROM SCRATCH, AS THERE ARE PLENTY OF EXCELLENT EDUCATORS LEADING WITH A.I. GO AND CHECK OUT SOME CASE STUDIES FROM THE UK-BASED WORKING GROUP AI IN EDUCATION, AI-IN-EDUCATION. CO.UK, WHICH ARE RELEVANT TO YOUR PROFESSIONAL PRACTICE. JOT DOWN THREE USEFUL IDEAS OR STRATEGIES YOU FOUND INTERESTING.

1.

2.

3.

KEY THOUGHTS FOR PROFESSIONAL PRACTICE

PLANTING SEEDS FOR THE FUTURE: A NEW MOVEMENT FOR CHANGE

As we bring this book to a close, let's end with some key thoughts to carry with us in our professional practice. Often innovation can be quite tribal, and people feel comforted by taking a singular stance in the face of change. I would argue that a more evolved and enlightened view is all about finding *balance*:

- We can be both pro-tech *and* pro-boundaries.

- We can both harness GenAI *and* be guarded about its risks.

- We can both be measured *and* agile in our approaches.

- We can both evangelise *and* be cautious.

- We can be both human-centred *and* technically engaged.

There are transformative, powerful benefits to learning from this new technology and we best serve our schools, our students and our collective futures by leveraging them to the best possible effect.

AFTERWORD

If this book has resonated with you and you'd like to learn more and connect with a community of teachers and leaders learning about AI, drop me a message with 'Join in' in the title at laura@sapio.company. I'd love to hear from you.

REFERENCES

CHAPTER 1

- Taylor, J. (2023) 'Rise of artificial intelligence is inevitable but should not be feared, "father of AI" says'. *Guardian*, 7 May. Available at: www.theguardian.com/technology/2023/may/07/rise-of-artificial-intelligence-is-inevitable-but-should-not-be-feared-father-of-ai-says

- The Growth Summit: Jobs and Opportunity for All (2024) *World Economic Forum*. Available at: www.weforum.org/events/the-growth-summit-jobs-and-opportunity-for-all-2023/

CHAPTER 2

- magicschool.ai, teacherbot.io, diffit.me and teachmateai.com (n.d.) *Various websites*. Available at: https://magicschool.ai, https://teacherbot.io, https://diffit.me, https://teachmateai.com

CHAPTER 3

- Inclusive Teach (2023) 'Examining the Principles of Inclusive Education in the UK'. Available at: https://inclusiveteach.com

- Schuelka, M.J. (2018) 'Implementing inclusive education', *K4D Helpdesk Report*. Brighton: Institute of Development Studies. Available at: www.gov.uk

- CAST, 'Universal Design for Learning Framework UDL: The UDL Guidelines'. Available at: https://cast.org
- gov.uk (2024) 'Initial Teacher Training and Early Career Framework'. Available at: www.gov.uk

CHAPTER 4

- Dellarocas, C. (2023) 'How GenAI could accelerate employee learning and development', *Harvard Business Review*. Available at: https://hbr.org (Accessed: 7 July 2024).
- Fayez, H. (2021) 'EEF Blog: Working with Schemas and Why it Matters to Teachers'. *Education Endowment Foundation*. Available at: https://educationendowmentfoundation.org.uk

CHAPTER 5

- Player, T. (2024) 'GenAI-at-Keble.pdf'. University of Oxford. Available at: https://ox.ac.uk (Accessed: 7 July 2024).
- GitHub (2024) 'Leaderboard Comparing LLM Performance at Producing Hallucinations when Summarizing Short Documents'. Available at: https://github.com/vectara/hallucination-leaderboard
- Good Future Foundation. Available at www.goodfuture.foundation/

CHAPTER 6

- UNESCO (2023) 'Artificial intelligence and the Futures of Learning'. Available at: https://unesco.org
- AI in Education 'Home'. Available at: https://ai-in-education.co.uk

INDEX